I Don't Know How I Know...
I Just Know

By: Gail Alexander

I Don't Know How I Know...I Just Know

copyright ©2016 by IbbiLane Press

All rights reserved. No part of this book may be reproduced or utilized in any form or by any means, electronic or mechanical, including photocopying, recording, or by any information storage and retrieval systems, without permission in writing from the publisher.

ISBN-13: 978-0692641859 (IbbiLane Press)

ISBN-10: 0692641858

This book is dedicated to all beings who have been
a part of my journey.
Thank You I Am Blessed.

Acknowledgements

First, I would like to thank my family.

I want to thank all of my friends. Your support, encouragement and belief in me is so appreciated. I could not be here without all of you.

To my friends Kammie and Kathy, you did a Herculean job. Grammar has never been my strong suit.

To Sue, thank you for supporting me and being an amazing sounding board when I needed one.

To Diane, for allowing me to use your sacred space on the water to start the process of transcribing and starting this book.

To Bill, Jennifer and Jodie, thank you for your honest feedback and encouragement helping me make this a better book.

To all of my teachers, I have learned so much from all of you.

To Kellie, for publishing this book and making this dream a reality.

To the reader, thank you for taking this journey with me.

Lastly, Thank you to my spirit team that guides, instructs, and supports me. I am extremely grateful.

Table of Contents

Introduction:	3
I don't know how I know . . . I just know	
Section One: The beginning	5
Growing up: How I learned to shut down and disconnect	6
The opening or re-opening depending on how you view it	15
What was I thinking?	26
Section Two:	31
Experiences, The good, the bad and the extremely strange and weird	32
Experiences in and around the akashic records	34
Experiences while driving or in vehicle	37
Experiences with Ancient Cultures	
Experiences in and around 911: How this event was pivotal to increase global consciousness	40
Experiences with mediums and medium-ship school this is going to be a doozy	43
Experiences with Reiki and Other Classes: meeting multi-dimensional beings while conscious	47
Experiences with Healing Sundays	50
Experiences at a Zen center	52
Section Three:	
Channelings and Experiences with Arch Angels, Ascended Masters, Light and Multi Dimensional Beings Oh My	53

Unicorn	54
Arch Angel Metatron	56
Mer People	58
The Elohim	61
Plato	62
Our Sun	63
Ascended Master Kuan Yin	64
Indigenous People of the Earth/Aborigines	65
Mary Magdalene	66
Ashtar of the Galactic Federation of the Light	68
Dolphins	70
Arch Angel Michael	72
Ascended Master St Germain	74
Ascended Master Jesus	75
Section Four: Meditations and Prayer	78
Chakra Wash	79
Chakra Triangle Meditation	82
Chakra Meditation with Mandalas	85
Meditation to get your own Symbol	94
Prayer to create own Symbol	96
Epilogue	97

Introduction: I don't know how I know... I just know

Where to start? This has always been the dilemma in creating this book. Do I start with my childhood and all my wacky experiences there? Do I start as an adult when all the gifts started to come back? This has been what has been holding me up. I don't know about you, but I have been feeling a lack of direction and overall malaise in my life. Over the last few years I have lost everything I believed to be important to me... my job, my money, and many friendships. The truth is I believe I have been on a pilgrimage over the last few years to completely rebuild my life and live up to my soul's potential.

At this time, I am being pushed by the universe, my guides, and teachers and loved ones (my spirit team) to write all of this down in a manner that makes sense to you the reader. Anyone else ever feel like you are being pushed? There is this pressure to get this done but I do not know why. They say hindsight is 20/20 so I am hoping when I am finished with this project it will make sense. I have started this book many different times. I was having a conversation with a friend and she said I don't know how I know, and I added I just know. This is how the title of this book was born. After that everything, else just fell into place and I was in flow. It made sense how to organize it and put it all together.

I am going on blind faith right now, which is really hard for me. There is and has always been a part of me that is extremely skeptical even though I know what I know. I am here to help humanity this I have always known. My spirit team works with me and gets me ready and then humanity makes different choices and I need to wait. I am done waiting. . . I am going to put this all out there for better or worse. I have been here on earth one way or another, every time humanity gets close to this point. I don't know about you but I would like to see us get it right this time and not have to start all over again.

I feel like my life is a science fiction movie. Sometimes I cannot even believe some of the things, situations and events that happen to me or that I have seen or been through. This is my journey through all of it. So fasten your seat belts . . . it is going to be a bumpy ride.

Like most kids I was extremely psychic. I had out of body experiences. I had energies in my room at night that communicated with me. I bi-located and I always knew when people were going to die. No one in my family wanted to hear about these things as it was a little frightening how accurate I was. So I closed down. More to come stay tuned.

I had a massive opening or I should say reopening to all my gifts. It started when I was in college and away from home. However, the really big event happened after I got divorced and took an opening to intuition course. You are not going to want to miss that chapter, as so much happened in that week. It really is unbelievable that I was not committed into a psychiatric facility. The good news for me during all of this was I am trained therapist so I was well aware that I was living in two worlds.

So, let's begin shall we. Welcome to my journey.

Section One:

The Beginning

Growing up: How I learned to shut down and disconnect

Much happened during my childhood and adolescence that caused me to want and start to shut down. I am going to skip around a great deal in this chapter because I want to represent the order in which the memories and situations came through for this book. So, this is the order I received the information internally as I wrote this.

I told my parents that my grandfather was going to die of a massive coronary; and sure enough, several weeks later he did have a massive coronary. He was on life support and everyone needed to decide what to do. I just remember him already having crossed over and was not in his physical body. I told everyone he already crossed over. This did not go over so well. It was clear my parents didn't want to know or didn't want to hear this from me.

My mother had been pregnant around this time. After returning from the hospital, she told us the baby was really sick and needed to stay in the hospital for a while. I put my arm around her and said, "the baby died why don't you just be honest mommy?" My mother left the room crying and I lost my mother emotionally that day.

I was always a challenge to my mother even when I was younger. My mother likes to say that even when I started talking at 9 months I was talking in complete sentences. Don't know if that is really true or not, but it does make a lot of sense knowing what I know. I guess I just wanted to get it all out and there was no time to waste.

We were at a museum and I got separated from my class. When my teacher frantically found me, I said, "what did you all get lost I have been sitting here waiting for you." My teacher was really mad. I calmly said, "I don't understand why you are so angry I wasn't lost and have been sitting here politely waiting for all of you to catch up . . ." This did not go over so well as you can imagine. Again clearly getting the message that no one really wants to hear what I had to say.

I was born with a lazy eye and could not even see the big E on an Eye chart but yet never bumped into anything. It was later in life that I came to understand why this was. I was using my third eye and not my physical human eyes to see. I felt much more comfortable in the spirit world than the physical world.

When I was younger I remember going to an eye specialist's office. One of the things that has stayed with me was the big round rug in the waiting room I had never seen such a big, round rug. The shape of the round rug changed the energy in the waiting room. I found this fascinating. I remember my parents and the doctor talking and discussing my options. Whether I was going to wear an eye patch or whether I was going to have surgery to correct my eye being so turned in. My parents said no to the surgery. I was shocked. I remember sitting there thinking, "isn't anyone going to ask me what I want it is my eye after all and affects me not them?" However, no one did; decisions were made for me. I quickly learned I did not get a say in what happens to me anymore, and was learning to shut down.

In first grade I wore an eye patch over my good eye so I could not really see much. It was physically uncomfortable to wear the eye patch with the adhesive. Every now and then in school I would cheat and peel it back so I could see and my teacher would scream at me. I just wanted to curl up and crawl under the desk. No one likes to be called out in front of the class and this was now becoming a daily occurrence. I didn't know what else to do as I couldn't see anything unless I pulled the eye patch back. I was in a no-win situation. I learned to not say anything yet again.

I had to have my tonsils and adenoids out while I was in Kindergarten because I could not breathe and eat at the same time and kept getting tonsillitis. I gained 10 pounds the first week and it did not stop there. I learned that if I ate and especially sugar, I could shut messages out.

All I remember when I was younger is I loved being outside in nature. Everything had a message and everything was alive and communicated. Why wouldn't you want to be a part of that? I was so connected and felt so alive that I never wanted that feeling to end. However, as the years progressed I stopped going outside all together. I found it difficult to live in the spiritual and physical world. I could not reconcile the two.

Soon I became allergic to the outdoors and rarely went outside anymore. I was allergic to every tree, grass, pollen, and flower. I believe this was my way of trying to protect myself. To this day, I still prefer to live in the spiritual world than the physical human world. It is so much easier. When I stand outside and connect to the spiritual world, I feel at peace and experience sense of belonging.

I gained more and more weight. As I gained the weight, my mother became more and more upset with me; constantly yelling at me and telling me she was going to wire my mouth shut. I continued to gain weight. I learned early on that my mom threatened a lot, but never followed through with it. My mother kept taking me to doctors and putting me on diets. The more my weight went up, the angrier she became with me. My mother just wanted me to be like all the other kids in the neighborhood. That was the one thing I was not willing to do. I knew I wasn't like them, and wasn't willing to try.

As the years of childhood went on, I became heavier and heavier, and more depressed. I stopped going to eighth grade because I was tired of being teased about my weight and thought school was stupid . ... It was not like I was learning anything that was going to actually help me. If there were school refusal programs at that time, I am sure I would have been placed in one. I was never fearful that I would not graduate, I just didn't want to be in school, and I had no problem with doing the work. The school also stated I needed to see the school social worker. This was completely ridiculous as all she did was offer me a piece of candy every time I went down there. We never actually talked about anything. No one ever asked me what was going on or why I was not going to school. Everyone just had meetings about me, and did not include me. I did not care for this approach. I was not going to volunteer anything unless someone asked me directly and no one ever did.

My mother and I played a game every morning. She would wake me up and I would pretend to be sleeping and then she would call me in sick . . . it worked every time because she felt so bad that I was so overweight. She let me get away with everything. The days I did go to school, I would go to the nurse and I always had just enough of a temperature to get sent home. I learned to actually raise my body temperature, as I hated school that much. I didn't know at the time, most kids put the thermometer under a light or arm to raise the temperature. I actually had learned to raise my body temperature; I discovered it was not really that difficult. I would have 99.6 every time at the nurse and that was enough to get sent home. My mom would get really frustrated as she would retake my temp a couple hours later and it was always normal. Everyone wanted to know what I was doing. I couldn't explain it back then.

Towards the end of the year, there was a meeting with my parents and the school principal. It was really uncomfortable in the meeting, where the principal stated he was going to come pick me up at my house if I did not come to school. You could not get away with saying that now or even doing that in today's day and age. I was also told what work I needed to make up in order to graduate with my class. I had never once thought I would not graduate. I did the work and stayed after school to get it done. The school also stated I need to see a psychologist. This was really stupid.

I went to see the psychologist ever week. I was not really forth coming with information. Besides, there was a drugstore in the building he was in. So, I was bribed with getting something every time I went for an appointment. It seemed to me that the psychologist did was play games with me every week and have me draw pictures. I understand now, as a therapist, that he was actually getting a great deal of information from me.

There is one memory that stands out very clearly to me. I was about 12 years old. I was at overnight camp. I was standing on the porch of one of the cabins and the next thing I knew is I was home playing with my friends. It was so clear I could remember the conversations and what we were playing, wearing and talking about. Then someone called my name and I jerked back into my body at camp. This is one of my first conscious episodes of bi-locating. I did not understand it at the time, and it was not something I was going to talk to anyone at camp about.

Another anomaly in my childhood was my room was always 15-20 degrees colder than anywhere else in the house. There was always so much energy in my room and I still had many friends who were coming to visit me even though I had decided to not stay conscious of it. I know they were watching over me and for this I am grateful. My room was my safe haven and still is to this day…

Growing up, my grandmother had a cottage on a lake. This was my safe haven. I loved being out on the water in the water anything to do with water. I could sit in the boat or just on the dock and I was very content. As I got older I stopped doing this, because it was too painful to be that connected. Again, I had to shut everything off in order to survive as a human being as my parents were not so keen on what I knew and how I knew it.

Childhood and adolescence were very rough for me. I grew up in the Jewish tradition and remember sitting in the synagogue on the highest of holiest days thinking this was really stupid and why did we need to go through an intermediary if we wanted to talk to g-d. Why didn't we just do it ourselves? The only thing that I did like about going to the synagogue was the energy that got created from the prayers and songs and everyone being one. That part of it was always amazing to me. When people come together for one purpose the energy that gets created is palpable.

I often times wondered how I got stuck in this family because it did not seem like I belonged in any way. I often times felt like a fish out of water. I wondered what I was thinking when I picked this family and these lessons. I wondered if I had somehow gotten in the wrong line or if this was all that was left. I know now that was not the case, my soul picked this opportunity and these circumstances to help me continue to grow and develop. Sometimes you just have to wonder though.

In sixth grade I started eye therapy for my lazy eye and needed to go a couple times a week. I was made to stand on something, balance and watch this thing going around in circles. I thought this was really stupid to say the least. Then they would have me close my eyes and put flashing strobe light up to my eyelids for 15 minutes because I never saw after-images. Well, let me tell you, all I see now is after images.

While in high school, my mom begged the school to put me in a special program to help with homework and studying. As we all know, I did not have such a good track record with school and homework. I was really rude during the interview process. However, my mother kept telling them I really needed to be in the program. Needless to say, they let me in the program. A couple days before high school started, we had to go take standardized tests. As this was not something that I really enjoyed, I made pretty geometric patterns out of the answer sheets. At the end of the school year, we had to retake the tests to see if we had improved. I know this is going to be hard to believe, but I was truly sick the week of the tests with a 101 fever. When I returned to school I took all the tests in two days that it took the other students took a week to do. I scored 12-plus on everything except math. This apparently was an outstanding score. The administrators were not amused that I had been in this program.

When I was 16, I was taken to a different therapist. This was one of my parent's friends who had become a therapist and wanted to work with me. When she met with me the first time, she asked me how I was feeling. I was in shock; no one had asked me that in so long. I did not answer or talk in therapy for a really long time. She was very patient with me and over time I started talking and started to deal with some of the issues from my childhood. As a therapist now, I think it is fascinating that I never had any family sessions. Again, this really highlighted and corroborated the point that there was something wrong with me; it was my issue not theirs.

There are many more examples or stories I could share where I was given the message that what I had to say was not important, and people were scared about what might say or know. I have come to peace with all that I have been through and have learned to use my voice to communicate again. It was a long process and has been an amazing journey. If I can leave you with one from this chapter, there is always hope and you can get through anything.

The opening or re-opening depending on how you want to view it

My journey began in an Opening to Intuition class. "Be Careful of Your Intentions and the Intentions of Others around You". I wanted my third eye to re-open in the class, and boy did it ever!

There were four students, the teacher and two teaching assistants. We all arrived during the day and class did not start until sundown that evening. We did a ceremony around a fire to start the class. It was very Native American shamanistic. After the ceremony was over, I closed my eyes for a minute trying to center myself and keep myself from freaking out. All of a sudden I felt this amazing golden light go all the way around my human body particularly my head. I was filled with the most peaceful, blissful feeling I could possibly describe to you. I heard a voice in my head say 'I am Mother Mary and I am here to help you'. That really freaked me out because that was the first time I heard a voice in my head talking to me other than my own. I chose not to share this experience with anyone because I did not know any of the other people and barely knew the teacher; I had only met her once.

After I opened my eyes from the golden light experience, I was staring the fire and the amazing colors and patterns of the flames were mesmerizing to me, I was in a trance. It was like I was one with the fire, then the next thing I know I saw a being in and around the fire and did not know who it was. The being introduced himself as Jesus, and did not look like any of the pictures I ever saw of him. Jesus started telepathically communicating with me and assuring me I was going to be okay. The message I received was that it was time for us to reconnect, that I had work to do and he would be with me while I did a lot of my work. I didn't understand why a Jewish girl from Skokie was seeing Jesus in the fire. Needless to say I was a little freaked out. My thought process at the time was if this was the first night of class, what the hell is going to happen tomorrow and the rest of the class? This went on for months; Jesus was with me everywhere I went and especially when I was learning. I came to be comforted by his presence and grace.

The lake house we were staying in had many different energies and forces in it; some might say it was even haunted. Needless to say, I did not sleep very much that first night or for the nights that follow. I remember thinking that night, as I was trying to sleep, what am I doing here? How did I get here? How can I leave without upsetting anyone? I just wanted to run away as far and as fast as I could. I felt like I was in way over my head and had no one to talk to. I was so scared and felt so alone.

The first day of class had arrived and passed; I managed to make it through the night in the haunted lake house. How I did that, I am not sure, because I remember my heart felt like it was pounding out of my chest all night. I do not remember what our first activities were; I do remember I had four bloody noses on the first day alone. I quickly learned by day two and more bloody noses, this was a by-product of being in state of being in a great deal of energy. This would be a sign I would learn to pay attention to as the years progressed. I always got bloody noses when something major was going to happen.

In the evening one night, the teacher told us we were going to have a healing night. The teacher had just gotten back from Brazil and John and G-d. We were told we would be doing healings similar to how they did them at the casa. We would all sit in the same room, she called it the 'current room', and we would go into a meditative state. Then, one by one, we would get called into the healing room for a healing. I was a little skeptical of all of this and was thinking to myself what the hell did I get myself into? Why am I here? I do not what to do this at all. I have already seen Mother Mary and Jesus and now I am going to do healing work. *I was like yeah right…*

Needless to say, we proceeded anyway. I chose to keep my fears and thoughts to myself, as no one else seemed to have any issues with it. So we started off in a group meditation. Meditation was still very new to me, it was not something I had ever done or practiced prior to this. This particular meditation was more to create a sacred space and raise the frequency and vibration in this haunted lake house. I felt a tap on my shoulder and I was taken into the room first, I think based on my level of skepticism. My teacher and her two assistants were all in the room dressed in white and I was told to lie down on the massage table. My heart was pounding out of my chest. I did not know what she was going to do, it was very frightening to me but I lay down on the table. I lay down on the table, my heart was pounding, my breathing was shallow and I was filled with fear and uncertainty. As I lay on the massage table, I could feel energy all around me, changing things in my energetic field. I was no longer scared. I could feel Jesus near by and I was no longer scared, and I was able to relax. I can remember my teacher talking, but have no idea what she was saying. It was like I entered a different time and dimension. I felt things swirl around me and then my teacher said, "you are done you can go back to the current room and go back into meditation". I was like, *that was not so bad.*

Once all the other people in the class were taken and brought back, I thought we were done. Then all of a sudden, I felt a tap on my shoulder and it was my teacher asking me to go back into the healing room. I followed her back in and then was completely unprepared for what I heard. My teacher said the teaching assistant needed a healing and I was to do it. I looked at her like she had lost her mind. What was she talking about? I was supposed to do what? She must have understood my look of total fear and confusion, because I then heard her say that I was just supposed to trust my hands would know where to go and what to do. The teaching assistant I was working with/on gave her permission. I took several deep breaths and then felt my hands moving and all kinds of energy come pouring through them. I heard many internal messages, but was uncertain if I was to say them aloud. When I was done I was even more petrified, scared and unsure of what had just happened. Once that experience was over it was time for bed and we did not process it in any way. I was left with more questions and more uncertainty and another sleepless night in the haunted house.

The next day we were doing a guided imagery activity and all of a sudden I could see and feel my third eye. I saw my third eye open, first there where swirling white lights then prismatic lights, then I could actually feel my third eye open and blink several times. Then I was transfixed by the beautiful, amazing and awe-inspiring images I saw. There was no turning back after this. I was on my mystical path that I had tried to block all my life up until this point.

After the swirling and blinking stopped, I saw Atlantis. It was amazing. I saw the city, the gate with 144 spheres, 72 on each side, forming a huge diamond at the top of the gate and the energy that it produced was breathtaking. I was shown the lab and able to play with all the technology. This has been a place that I frequently go when I do meditations now. There is a reason I love new gadgets and technology so much.

The next stop on the third eye opening adventure was the pyramids all over the earth, how they were built and our relationship with nature. We worked so closely with nature, sound and vibration then. The stones were set in place from above and hovered over the correct coordinates before being placed. Of course, we had some help from above as well. This was again awe inspiring to witness, and the personal history lesson I was downloaded with at the time was amazing. I got flooded with information; it just kept coming and coming and coming, kind of like the energizer bunny. I did not know how to stop it.

The next stop on the third eye opening adventure was Double Helix DNA and genetic disorders. I had no idea what I was seeing as my highest level of science was biology-based one. I was shown how DNA strands were formed the different patterns they break into and the many unique combinations that make us up. The combinations were in patterns of 8, 12, 32, 64, etc. I didn't know what that was because I had never seen it before, but I was able to explain it and talk about it like I had studied it all my life. I could explain why we have genetic disorders, where the tears in the DNA strands were and what needed to be created and developed to see them and repair them.

Up until this point in my life math and science have never been my strong suit. The highest math class I had was algebra and geometry. Now here I am seeing ancient cultures, technologies, and even DNA with no reference point, but can describe it in great detail. I saw genetic disorders tools to discover them, all kinds of healing arts. I asked so many questions that day and disrupted the whole class that the instructor banned me from asking anymore questions until the last day of class. Once again, I felt like I did not fit in, like no one wanted to hear what I had to say, to try to understand my experience. Even in a metaphysical class I was still different then everyone else and my peers in the class were frustrated with me as to why I was having this transformational experience and seeing all these things and they were not. I chose to stop talking in the class after that unless asked a direct question after an activity and gave very brief answers or left information out. I did not want to make it harder for anyone else. However, the more activities we did the more information I started to get, the more questions I had and the more information I continued to get. I felt like I was on a never-ending roller coaster and did not know how to exit the ride. So I kept my hands and feet in the vehicle until it finally came to a stop holding on for dear life.

Here I was having this very metaphysical experience I had asked for, was completely ungrounded with a teacher who wanted to see what else I could do and how high I could go. I was processing and holding so much energy and was not aware of what to do with it and how to process it. Yet no one wanted to answer my questions or hear what I had to say.

Next stop or activity was my experience with the Lords of the Akashic Records. The Akashic Records are the books of our soul's life. One of the teaching assistants was a trained akashic record reader and gave us a brief overview and then we each got to have a 20-minute session. I had never heard of the Akashic Records before this point, but the more we talked about it the more images I kept receiving about the records and the Lords. When I walked into the room she was doing the readings in, I could see the Lords of Akasha all lined up and feel the power of the books of life. I had always had the sense I was killed by a guillotine and died in the concentration camps. So when it was my turn to have my records accessed, the person doing the reading said they normally do not answer questions like this because of free will. I already knew the answers in my heart, but the Lords of the Records, The Ascended Masters and my Loved Ones, said they want me to know the answer was yes, because then you will have an easier time trusting the information that you get. That was true, once that was confirmed for me; I did relax a little bit. Again this experience proved be no different, I was taken on Mr. Toads Wild Ride. I could actually see the

Lords of Akasha, I could see the hall of records. I knew what the person reading my records was going to say before she did. One of the things I saw again was a gate. This time I was swimming underwater with dolphins and other blue phosphorous beings. I was taken to this gate and told my hand would open it. I put my hand up on the scanner-like device and sure enough, the gate opened. It was an amazing city. I had completely forgotten about this until years later when dolphins, whales and mermaids came to visit me.

As a group one afternoon we went into town and out to lunch. I wanted to drive my car. I thought that would be fun. Everyone just looked at me and laughed. They all said, "I am not getting in a car with you – you are not grounded at all!" Well, I went with someone else and then had another experience. While we were walking into the restaurant I looked down at my hands and they were not my physical hands plus they were holding something and I was not. When I looked up, I realized I was not looking out my eyes. Someone was in my body with me using my body to look at humanity. I am still not completely sure who it was; but it was either Mother Mary or Isis that entered my body that day. They were holding a rosary or ankh. Again let me remind you of the whole Jewish thing – this was way out of my experience and comfort zone. I was so freaked out I don't think I said a word during lunch.

When we got back from lunch my teacher told me to go out on the pier and be grounded by the water. Well, being the somewhat spoiled and materialistic individual I was at this time, I took my cell phone, mp3 player and any other distraction I could think of at this time. After a few minutes of playing with all that stuff I decided to just lie down on the pier and close my eyes. I was not prepared for what happened next. I started to see all of these white birds circling around my head. I would open my eyes and there would be one or two in the physical sky. I would close my eyes and there would be hundreds of white birds, they were everywhere. I got frightened and went inside to find my teacher because I did not know what else to do. I knew she was not going to be helpful and I also knew I could not stay outside any longer.

My teacher asked me why I was back so soon. I explained what happened with the white birds over my head and she was not surprised and really annoyed with me. She couldn't even leave you alone to do anything without something happening. I felt so bad. I was not trying to bother anyone; I was just so scared and felt so alone while having this amazing metaphysical experience that everyone else so desperately wanted to have. My teacher explained white birds represented lost souls and they could all see me and wanted me to help them. I said help them with what? My teacher explained they wanted me to help them cross over. At this point I began to feel like I did not fit in anywhere. Here I was in a class with people to open your intuition, but mine was apparently on full throttle, and the teacher was not able to help guide, protect or understand me.

On one of the last evenings of the class we were told we were going to create gift mandalas for each other. We drew names and the more and more I thought about this activity, the more I started to panic and this over whelming fear came over me.

For some reason leaving did not seem like a viable option so I did the next best thing I could think of to save myself. I threw a temper tantrum and repeated over and over again, I can't draw, you can't make me do this, and I refuse. The teacher was having none of it, and although I held the class up for over 45 minutes, I ended up doing the activity. The fear of doing this activity was palpable; it came from a place so deep inside myself. Again my teacher was neither compassionate nor caring, and basically told me I needed to suck it up and do it. We were lead into a guided imagery to meet the guide of the person we were to create the image for as a gift. All went smoothly on that part. I was now much more comfortable with meditation. When I looked down at the image I had created it was unlike any other in the room. Mine was this precise image designed for a specific purpose. The more I looked at it, I realized that the image brought forth was to help balance this individual's lazy eye and was scientific down to the colors and patterns. The person I created it for was under-enthused that he did not receive what he was hoping for in his gift. Yet again, I felt terrible that mine was different and wondered what I was doing wrong.

Drawing mandalas has turned out to be one of the greatest gifts I ever received. Moving past this fear has literally changed my life. I have not stopped drawing since that fateful night. I have created over 3000 images and have infused many pieces to help people recover and bring themselves into balance.

It was time to say goodbye. Class was over. It was time to return to my regular life. I had to go back to my new job that I had started three weeks prior. I did not know how I was going to manage this. I was ungrounded and still on Mr. Toads' wild ride. The teacher informed me she was repeating the one-week intensive class over a 12-week period and recommended I go through the class again. This sounded like a good idea. I thought it would help me integrate all of the experiences. Boy was I wrong about that. 12-weeks turned into 16-weeks. The mystical experiences kept coming and coming. Kind of like the energizer bunny.

What was I thinking?

I was curious about so much after my re-opening experience. Windows and doors were flying open. Here are some of the things I was curious about during this time. Hopefully, it will help you start to think about all these things for yourself, and what is important to you on your journey. I think one of the biggest things I have learned over the years is we all have our own unique individual journey. However there are some similar themes that we all experiences as humans.

What does life mean? Why are we all here? What lessons do we need to learn, relearn and keep learning? How do we learn to balance all of it? What is the payoff? What is being alive? What does that really mean?

These are the answers that came through:
- Sometimes it is an amazing beautiful, incredible, joyful process, and sometimes it is painful, scary and overwhelming
- Just allow yourself to be in the moment that is what it is all about.
- Just be yourself.
- Do not take yourself too seriously.
- Learn to relax, play and laugh.
- This is such a short experience in the grand scheme of things.
- Enjoy it while you are privileged enough to have it.
- Remember to breathe.
- Slow down every day and to go within.
- Connect with the divine.
- Live your life as you are meant to live it.

- Trust yourself enough to do that.
- Have faith that everything will work out as it is meant too.
- Trust that there are no accidents only choices and directions.
- Be free, be happy and most important just be.
- Do not be afraid of who you are.

Trust means having faith. Trust means taking that blind leap. Trust means giving up the control you think you have. What happens when you do this? What happens when you follow your hearts desire and take the leap? Why do so many of us struggle with faith? Why is it such a hard thing to accept? What I love?

These are the answers that came through:
- Faith is a way to connect with the universe.
- Faith is one of the most beautiful things in the universe.
- Faith gives us a sense of belonging.
- Faith gives us a sense everything will be okay.
- Faith is a way to make the ordinary extraordinary.
- Losing faith sets one down the path of darkness, the path to despair and depression.
- Reconnecting with faith and all that is – is going to be what gets you through.
- There is no fear in having faith and believing.
- Love is what connects us to each other.
- Believe. Have hope. Have faith
- Follow your own path.

- Connecting is so natural, so incredible and so blessed.

Why do people invent so much, like addictions, diseases and loneliness? When will people in this world realize we all need each other? When will people of the world learn to be kind, compassionate and generous with themselves and others? How do you know when you are truly alive? What does that feel like?

These are the answers that came through:
- Being alive is consciously seeing what your choices are
- Being awake is seeing the possibilities of your choices.
- Be mindful of joy.
- Just take a minute to stop and just experience the majesty of all that is.
- Learn how to quiet the mind.
- Unplug every now and then and just be.

Everyone in the world has his or her own unique talents, gifts and essence to share. Have we become so technological that we have lost the ability to connect with ourselves let alone truly connect to anyone else?

These are the answers that came through:
- Take time every day to center your self and go within.
- Ask yourself everyday do I consciously chose life?
- Make life-affirming decisions.
- The choice is yours.

- Chose wisely because the choice affects the path you will walk.
- Reaching for the light.
- Fear is the only thing that can get in your way.
- Encourage and allow yourself to sit quietly and center yourself everyday.
- Believe in yourself.
- Everyone can feel oneness. It is available to all.

What if we create our own suffering? What if our thoughts and emotions have more affect on our human bodies and energy systems than we currently think?

These are the answers that came through: More questions:
- If this is indeed the case then what will healing look like in the future?
- If disease affects more than the human body then how can medicine (pills) or drugs cure or release the illness from the body?
- As human beings we are more than a physical body, we have many layers, and illness can affect all of these layers.
- How can something designed to cure just the physical part actually heal an illness?
- What if the medicine in the future takes the body, mind, soul, spirit and energy of the person into account?
- What if how we currently treat things is actually barbaric . . . what then?
- When do we stop letting big business control how we heal?

This is not going to be a popular view. However, I believe we need some fresh perspectives and new ways to look at things. What if a multi-disciplinary treatment team consists of western doctors, *and* metaphysical healing practices and even spiritual leaders? Addressing all aspects of the individual, not just the physical body and the mind?

I think this about covers the ramblings and questions that have come up for me thus far on the journey. I am sure it brings up questions for you? Maybe it is time to start having conversations about the things we are really curious about. Stop pushing aside your questions because of how other people may feel or because you are too afraid you may be judged.

Section Two:
Experiences: The Good, The Bad, The Extremely Strange and Weird

Experiences in and around the Akashic Records

One time when I was in my akashic records, a whale came in and was communicating with me. I felt such joy and such peace with this being. All I wanted to do was play. At one point the whale brought in his baby and we were all playing in the water like we were old friends. It was an amazing, out of this world experience. When it was time for the whales to leave I started sobbing. I remember repeating I am not leaving and they are not leaving me.

In the beginning I used to see 100s of faces before I went to sleep. One night as I was falling asleep, a young Peruvian boy came to visit me and said he needed me to come with him and the older gentleman with him. It had appeared as they had traveled for some time to reach me. I said that I was really tired and needed to get some sleep. I offered to help them at another time.

A few days after this, I was in my akashic records again when the Peruvian boy and older gentleman returned. It seemed rather urgent and they were insistent that I help them this time. I said that I would go with them. They took me to the Andes mountains where all the planes crash. I said I could clearly see what the problem was. Since I am one of the crystal keepers of the earth, I realized that someone had moved the crystals in the mountains. I worked with their help to realign all the crystals. I have not heard about any more crashes since then.

I digress here for a moment because this reminds me of another experience. When I was working with my akashic record teacher, I started to see rainbow light shooting out my hands. I could make all these really cool rainbow bridges. It felt amazing. I did not know why or how I was able to do this, I just was. It wasn't until I took Ancient Rainbow Conscious Healing that I understood about the rainbow light. During Ancient Rainbow Conscious Healing you learn to work with the rainbow light from Lemuria.

Experiences While Driving or In Vehicles

There would be times when I was driving in my car and could see and feel a unicorn herd around me going with me everywhere I went. This was a slight departure and major energy change from the mutli-dimensional beings that were already traveling with me.
One of the other really fun experiences is when I had three travelers in my back seat that went with me everywhere I went. Some of my friends could even see them and feel them...

Often times my spiritual experiences seem to correlate to what is happening with and on the earth. I was on a vacation with some friends in the boundary waters of Minnesota. I knew it was going to be an interesting trip because as soon as we turned off the paved roads onto the gravel the adventure began. I looked out the window and it was not just trees anymore. Everything was just energy, with no real form or shape. Then I looked over at my friend who was driving and it was like being in the movie the matrix. When I looked at my friend, I did not see her physical body. I saw her energy field and all that was going on in her body.

That is not the first time this has happened to me. I have learned to pay attention when something like this happens. All of a sudden after looking at my friend for a while, the images switched to seeing earth energy. I became part of the living grid and was in the hologram riding all the ley lines. I saw all the energy moving across the earth and then it just stopped when it got to England. I did not understand what that meant. Several days later I heard what happened when the bombers tried to board the plane in London. Then it made sense as to why the energy of the ley lines stopped there. Now the problem becomes what do I do with this kind of information when I get it?

Some of the other experiences I have had while driving are a bit different. I have had entire meditations given to me while I was driving my car. I was also given a lecture on chakras and colors and how they intermix. Another experience on a road trip was, I was speeding and two hundred feet in front of my car two birds landed on the road ahead. I was forced to slow down quickly to avoid hitting them, and then they flew away. Another hundred feet in front of the birds was a police officer waiting to give a speeding ticket? Thank you for the help in avoiding that one.

I received information and images of a learning center while driving. The structure was made of an opaque material I had never seen before. The structure consisted of three levels in the shape of the infinity symbol. The top level was a high tech communication hub where much time was spent. 15 years after receiving the original information I learned this structure was actually from Lemuria. I was shown the structure to help me learn how to communicate on multi-dimensional levels I took many classes there in meditation. Wow, if that is not a star trek moment I don't know what is. Again, just one of many. Ironically, we give more credence to those sci-fi shows than we do to the possibility of these experiences happening here and now. What odd creatures we are. We'll grant that there may very well be other beings and civilizations "out there", but when faced with something we don't understand in the here and now, we certainly won't consider those possibilities as realistic.

Experiences with Ancient Cultures

I have also had dreams of underwater cities that still exist on the earth right now. Sometimes, I have a hard time when I am by water because I am so connected to all of them. Although I love being by or on water, It is hard to get me to go in water. Once I am in the water I never want to come out.

While I was in meditation one day, I was called on to fix the broken, misfiring Atlantean beam. Any guesses where this beam was? If you guessed the Bermuda Triangle, you are right. This beam had been misfiring for years. It is not that planes, boats and submarines disappeared they were simply transported into another dimension.

One of the other visitors I had frequently in the beginning where the Priestess of ISIS or as I have always referred to them as the Women in White robes. The Priestesses of ISIS were not of human decent. They were the star seeds or co-creator G-ds that were left here to help humanity. Sometimes they had a hard time with the limitations of being in the denseness of the third dimension. The true intent of Egypt was to build another society like Atlantis and Lemuria, but things got lost in the translation so to speak. The masculine and feminine were out of balance and this was the beginning of the more masculine energy taking over on planet earth. More of the negative side of Atlantis got translated in Egypt and the misuse of power, and technology became rampant as a result.

Speaking of the Priestesses of ISIS, this is going to be a hard one for a lot of people to swallow. Some of the information I received is that Jesus did not die on the cross, "nearly dead" like in the movie The Princess Bride. He was taken down as there were dignitaries coming into town. He was taken into a cave where the Priestesses of ISIS were and restored to health where he walked out. I am not sure how I even feel about this one, but it felt like important information to share.

My meditations have shown me the Sphinx and the pyramids of Giza. The original pyramids look much different than today, and the capstone (crystals) were buried in the Giza compound. These crystals are red, yellow and green. Red means stop. Stop also means not being connected to the earth and the rhythms of the earth. Yellow means slow down, so not really wanting humans to be in their power. Green means go about being heart-centered. My meditations taught me that there are many messages left for humanity to decode if we are willing to look and understand their meanings.

The pyramids were healing pyramids they were beautiful and powerful. When you entered, you would levitate close to the top and the energies would come down from above through the massive crystal and the earth energies would come up from below balancing the person out. Kind of like Leonardo Da Vinci's drawing of man with arms and legs apart. Each person would be given the energy that they needed. After awhile humans started to become afraid and belief systems changed. Fear started to creep in and this was the beginning of the end.

The beings that came through think it is really funny, that we humans believe the pyramids were built by slaves. Early on in my learning journey, I learned that humans had a very different relationship with nature and our environment (physical world). If a piece of stone was asked to move to certain coordinates, it would be levitated and moved with frequency and vibration. Of course there was some help from *above* or *beyond our world*, as well.

Experiences in and around 911: How this event was pivotal to increase global consciousness

This is a difficult topic to talk about because it brings up so much for so many people. However I think it is important to talk about my experiences associated with 911. A couple of weeks before 911 happened, I had decided to try acrylic painting – just seemed like a good idea at the time. Turned out painting was not my strong suit and I chose to stick to mandalas.

One night the week before 911 happened I was coming home from work during twilight. My drive home was about 45 minutes. There was an absolutely beautiful, amazing and huge pink cloud with me my entire drive home. I became obsessed with this cloud and decided to paint it the Sunday (before 911). Again painting not my strong suit, but I recreated it the best I could and then put it away. I really didn't think anything else about the painting or the pink cloud again. Like everyone else, I was in total shock and awe of the events that took place on that day.

I was working in a Behavioral Health Hospital at this time and did not have any access to a television all day. This for me was a great thing, as I could not see the images or feel the energy. Remember that part about me being intuitive? Well it turns out I did not need a TV to see what was happening. I could see, feel and hear the terror of the people in the towers and the ones who jumped off. This is yet another vision that is forever etched in my brain. Sometimes I am not sure if it is always a gift to be so intuitive. Sometimes I think it is a curse, as you can feel so connected to all that is happening you feel like you are losing yourself. I am sure people reading this have felt this way one time or another.

When I got home and saw the actually image, I talked with some of my friends who were also intuitive. I started to realize that all these individuals who lost their lives on that day, did so to help the rest of us who are still here move forward and help humanity to survive. Looking back on this event now, it is by far the biggest shift in human conscious to this point. This event and tragic events that happen all over the world help connect or reconnect us to our humanity and remember we are all one and live in one world albeit divided it is the same planet. We as human beings took a big leap that day into true global consciousness.

The hospital I worked at had a memorial service and I could feel the energy as we all came together as one. All I could see and feel was Kwan Yin and her arms reaching out to us to help us all heal with compassion. It felt like the world was being held in a huge hug.

Then I got flooded with information. What is my responsibility to pass this information along and then whom to pass it along too without sounding crazy? This has always been part of the dilemma for me. As I was working in mainstream behavioral health hospitals what is going too far? Again, this is kind of ironic as our religious-based organizations ask us to believe in beings who foretold of events and engaged in behaviors that don't seem based in reality or even science?

Months later when I pulled out that painting I did the Sunday before the disaster, that I realized I had painted the explosion. The top of the painting was grey with lighting bolts and the bottom of the paining was the blue water. The explosion was the big pink cloud that I saw. Again, thank you to all the beautiful souls that signed up to help us make the transition and open our perception. I am grateful to each and every one of you.

Here is the painting I did a week before 911 happened. I am not the best painter in the world I will stick with mandalas. I think it is important to give you the visual of what came through.

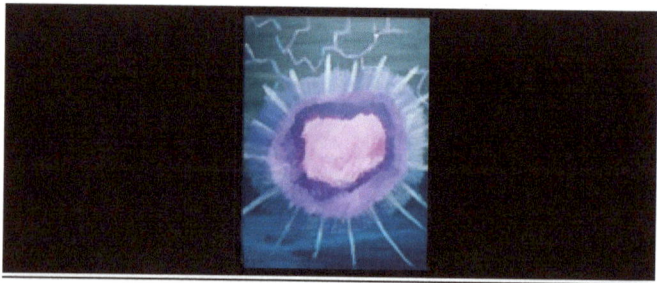

Experiences with mediums and medium-ship school... this is going to be a doozy...

Over the years, I have had the pleasure of meeting and experiencing many mediums. I have at times channeled information through my mandalas and readings. For some reason I was called to attend medium-ship school one summer. In retrospect, I am not sure if I was actually being called to go to medium-ship school or if the instructor, called me to see what would happen. I was in no way prepared for what was about to happen to me and come through me.

I was very naïve in the beginning of my journey and blankly trusted everyone who seemed to know things I did not. These were people who had been on the path a lot longer than I had. I believed they were of the light and would be able to help and guide me. Most of all I thought they had my best intention in mind. This did not turn out to be true.

The second day of medium-ship school we were all going to get a chance to channel and help spirits who were stuck cross over into the light. I watched others go through the process in the morning. That didn't sound so bad; I figured there was a room full of people that if something were to happen it would be okay.

I don't know about you when you take classes, but I sometimes get a little high from all the energy. I have had teachers tell me over and over that I need to eat a vegetarian diet to help keep energy high. Any higher, I would need to be scrapped off the ceiling. We took a break for lunch I had beef and caffeine in an attempt to ground myself so I would not go off into the ethers.

Now back from lunch and what I thought to be a grounding and dense meal, it was now my turn to take my place at the table and channel. I was a little nervous knowing what has happened to me in other classes. The instructor took us on a guided imagery and then I saw an older woman waiting. Archangel Michael told me this woman needed help to cross over. I thought this wasn't going to be so bad.

Then my mind went blank and black. Before I knew it the floodgates opened and I saw hundreds of thousands of people waiting to cross over. The first group I saw was from 911, there were all these hands reaching out to me. My body became a human ascension cone. I did not know what was happening. Once that group crossed, then I saw all the people from the Gulf War, the same scenario happened. At this point my physical body was having a hard time with all the energy. I started shaking and was almost in convulsions. I could feel the other students in the room and then heard the instructor say they could not help me. The instructor informed them this this needed to happen and not to interfere. After all the people from the Gulf War went through me, I saw all the people from the Tsunami. At this point I thought I was going to have a heart attack and die. I was sobbing uncontrollably my physically body shaking and now convulsing, and no one would help me. Finally by some miracle one of my hands was placed over my crown chakra and my other hand placed over my third eye chakra. After a few minutes of my hands on my crown and third eye chakras the energy, sobbing and convulsions eased up and I started to come back to the present moment.

To this day I am still haunted by these visions and all the people who needed to cross over. When I asked the instructor why she did not stop what was happening? The instructor said "I wanted to see what would happen it was no big deal; she had once had an experience like that once". I assured her it was a big deal and left. I felt scared, vulnerable, frightened and ashamed as to what I had just been through in front of other people. I felt very alone. I did not finish the class and did not attend the last day. I did go back to attend the graduation of my friends from the class. I personally, had no desire to finish.

It took me years to work through this. I wanted nothing to do with channeling or bringing messages forth or being intuitive for several years. This experience scared the crap out of me and I did not know what to do to move forward. To this day I am still a little skittish to channel. The only time I am really comfortable with channeling is when I am drawing or writing the messages to go with the mandalas.

I worked with a different channeling instructor years later. I knew I needed to get passed this fear and blocks that were created during medium-ship school. I felt safe to do this now. I trusted my spirit team. I knew they would not allow me to ever be in that position again. Later in the book I will share many of the channeled messages I have received.

Experiences with Reiki and Other Classes: meeting multi-dimensional beings while conscious

Another interesting experience is when I took Reiki, which was in the first year of my journey. We were having our attunements, which allow your energy to connect to the universal energies on the mental, physical, emotional and psychic level. I saw greyish, greenish, and bluish iridescent beings as clearly as I see human beings. I had never seen anything like this. The interesting thing is I was not scared. I felt peaceful. Later, I came to learn this was my first conscious experience with the Pleiadians. The Pleiadians are thought to be fifth dimensional multi-dimensional beings. They have been my guides for a long time. Since Pleiadians are used to driving crafts or ships, sometimes, they would drive me home from classes when I was not grounded. I always managed to make it home safely.

I found that in whatever class I took after Reiki, I was meeting new multi-dimensional beings. In Angelic Healing Fire, I met all the angels and ascended masters. This is also when Ashtar of the Galactic Federation of the Light came in to my awareness. I also formed a very strong relationship with Arch Angel Metatron at this time. In Ancient Rainbow Conscious Healing, I connected with the Rainbow People and saw many of my lifetimes in Atlantis and Lemuria. In DNA Theta healing I had more experiences with people who had crossed over. In the Akashic Records I met the Lords of the Records guarding the records. It was amazing. I had already had experiences with Jesus and Mother Mary from my opening to Intuition course. The floodgates were not wide open, and each class I took brought new experiences and challenges.

I also had to learn to navigate my teachers in all of these classes. A number of my teachers were intimidated by me or did not know what to do with me. Often times, they would ask me why I was taking their class. I was told they were worried as to how the other participants would feel with me in the class. I would explain, sometimes to fully incorporate something, there is a re-remembering or integration that needs to take place. This is what they classes represented to me.

I really frustrated my quantum touch instructor. In the first ten minutes of class, I was able to explain how quantum touch worked. I still had two more days of class to sit through. That was a challenge. I learned to become quiet in classes and try not to be a disruption as that is what I was told I was often.

I learned about psychometry in one class and everyone put an object in the bag so you did not know whose you were getting. I, off course, pulled the teachers item. I knew it was
hers right away and got flooded with information. When we went around to tell the class what

information we got from the object, she asked me not to share in front of everyone.

When I took theta healing, I had done so much work with my third eye and holding the energy for the class that my third eye was wide open and blown up. My teacher let me walk out the door in this shape, as she found me to be an annoyance. Her words to me were, "you know how to fix it anyway; I have other people to deal with." *Thanks a lot.*

I also had a hard time staying with meditations and was always ahead of where the rest of the class was. This really frustrated a number of my teachers. I guess there is a point where sometimes the student is the teacher and my teachers did not want to learn from me. All of these experiences in classes shaped how I feel about teaching and the responsibility I feel when I work with people.

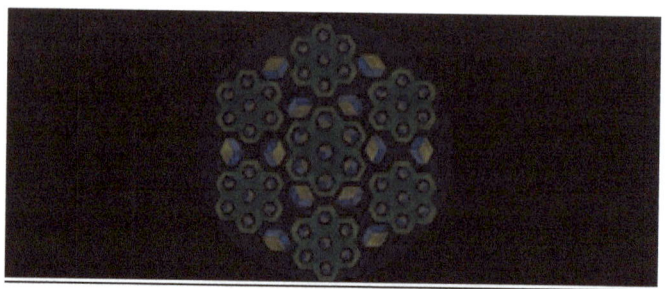

Experiences with Healing Sundays

So after completing opening to intuition twice, the teacher now recommended that I attend Healing Sundays at her center. The healings were set up in a similar way as the healings at the Casa in Brazil by John of G-d are arranged. These experiences became very similar to the experiences I talked about in the opening chapter. I went every Healing Sunday. I was never attached to where I was placed; I really just wanted to be of service. I would go into a really deep meditation and sometimes have no idea where I went or what happened.

This is a prayer I wrote that was used on Healing Sundays. This is for people to write their intention on the back to be read aloud, if getting a healing or put in a pile to do remote healings.

> Prayer: May you be blessed with divine grace, love and light to fill your heart. Spirit and soul for now and always. May the universe and creation carry you through every day. May you learn to see the beauty and lessens in all that surrounds you.
> Gail Alexander

As I attended more and more healing Sundays, I would get called to attend to the person lying on the massage table. It was an amazing experience, the individual would lie down on the table and I would see it as a CAT scan machine. Wherever there was a block or concern, it would light up. I knew exactly what needed to be done; I just let go and trusted. I was in an altered state most of the time. After the sessions were over I usually had no sense of what had happened or what I had done until others started talking about it.

It was during this time I had to deal with my fears around touching people. I always felt like the energy I carried was too strong. I would see white light shoot out from my hands. I did not want to hurt anyone. I never put my hands directly on anyone after that first night in opening to intuition class. I placed my hands a couple inches above their physical body to work on the individual's etheric field.

I felt such a rush from doing the healing work; it was such an amazing space to be in. There are times now that I really miss this. I still dome healing work on friends and clients occasionally. My focus has been more on mandalas and messages as of late. There will be a time when I will be able to go back to the healing work.

Experiences at a Zen Center

I went to a Zen Center. I had one of the most profound experiences on my journey at this time. We were all chanting and I could feel myself going into higher realms. The next thing I remember is being on the sacred mountain in Tibet having an ancient tea ceremony with Buddha, Jesus and Kuan Yin. I was welcomed back and imparted much information. Mostly, I just remember the feeling of being in profound unconditional love.

This experience was so profound. I felt a connection to the woman leading the chanting and service. This woman had converted from Judaism and I identified with her. I asked if I could call her and talk with her over the phone. She agreed and about a week later I had my appointment. I was so excited to talk with someone I felt such a strong connection with. Imagine my dismay when she kept asking me about my mental health. She kept telling me I really needed to get help that I was unstable. I explained that I was a mental health professional. I asked her about the goal of mediation. She said "to become one with everything". I said that is what I am telling you happened to me. She did not want to discuss it any further. I was at a loss as to what to do next.

Section Three: Channelings and Experiences with Arch Angels, Ascended Masters, Light and Multi Dimensional Beings Oh My

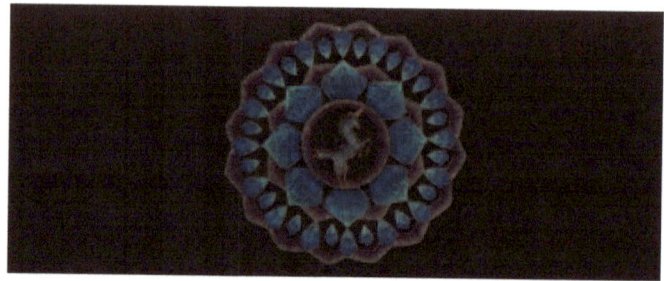

Unicorns

I have had the pleasure to connect with unicorns many times and it has always been delightful. This connection brings me joy and a smile to my face. Right now our frequency as human beings is not high enough for the unicorns to reappear as they are solely about joy and fun.

This is the message that came through:
We are the unicorns. We have created rainbow bridges with joyful energy to slide along to come and share our message. We bring more peace, knowledge and joy. I am the unicorn king. I have more of a male presence. We want and need humans to be more joyful and light filled so we can come visit more often. We are seventh dimensional beings who come to help those filled with joy. It is through our horns we project sparkly rainbow energy. We are iridescent in actuality in different light we project different colors. Most of the time you humans see us as white as that was what was depicted in many pictures and myths left behind for you. The unicorns will be returning to the earth plane when the energy gets higher, cleaner and more pure. There have been more sightings of us. We are attempting to come back but it is not quite

time. Again the energy of the planet and human beings needs to be higher, more pure and more joy filled.

We are slowly reintroducing ourselves again to humanity. We are showing her what we truly look like; which are beings of light and not as humanity has depicted us in the past. Connecting with us feels very much like being in oneness.

We, the unicorns, send love, light, joy and peace and wish to connect more. When you are laughing or filled with joy we will be there.

Again bringing them forth brought joy, peace and smiles. It was a true pleasure and honor.
Sometimes, when I am driving my car and I am in a playful mood, I can feel a herd of unicorns traveling with me. It is an unbelievable feeling.

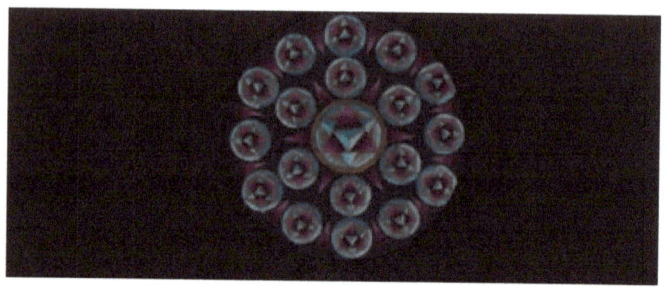

Arch Angel Metatron:

Arch Angel Metatron is a teacher of esoteric knowledge and sacred geometry. No surprise that he is one of my main guides. When I channel Arch Angel Metatron is one of my gate keepers who allows the other light beings and multi dimensional beings to come through. When Arch Angel Metatron is around I feel and see magenta and turquoise, this is how I identify it is him.

This is the message that came through:
The time of darkness and sadness on earth is over. Things need to get lighter. People must get lighter and be more joy filled. People must remember who they are and why they are here. Many will not be taking this journey on earth again. For many humans, this will end your lifetimes on earth as human beings.

Spiritual and esoteric learning is more than just concepts, algorithms and formulas. It is about bridging, and connecting. As science continues to move forward, humans are starting to see that everything is really alive and will be more able to prove the connections.

Channeling is not as difficult as humans make it out to be. Channeling is really the simplest form of communication there is. Often times as human beings, you talk and you don't know what you are going to stay next but trust that the information will come because on some level you know it. You don't always see or know the end goal when you start talking sometimes it is called brainstorming. This information is comes from somewhere. Channeling is about opening up and allowing. Everything is communicated in symbols. In the universe, all languages of earth are symbols; again humans need to broaden their thought process and expand their minds. Channeling is about connecting your soul, heart and human brain.

Mer People

I have recently reconnected with the mer people or what we humans refer to as mermaids or mermen. When I connect with them, there is a sense of floating and being timeless. It is always serene and I feel like I am delving deep into human consciousness. I am always left with a feeling of awe. I think of the mer people as the angels of the sea or the angels beneath.

This is the message that came through:
I do not have a name that she can pronounce. It is more a series of sounds we transmit to her when we call her. I am one of the mer people. It is hard for us to come up here. Usually we bring her down to us. It has taken awhile for us to figure out how to communicate using her vocal chords, air and sound. Her lungs hurt, as we are not used to breathing like this. We breathe fluidly in the water, and it is very different. We are all one. Some of us got curious to live on the surface of the planet. Part of the consciousness remembers. You can accept whales and dolphins yet, you struggle with accepting mer people as real.

When you are born you are in a womb full of fluid. You don't breathe air. You get all your nutrients from the fluid. It isn't until the baby is born and comes out that it takes its first breath of air and gasps. This is how you all came out of the water. In the beginning, it was really hard and you have forgotten what it was like. This is why there is such a fascination with water.

All the sonar technology is destroying us. All the things you will not do on your land you seem to think it is okay to do in your water. You need water to live and for us to survive. We watch over you and we hold your consciousness from below. We are coming around more for you to be in flow and in the moment. And not plan so much. Fluidity is the key to moving forward. There is one thing we want to leave you with. We are the angels of the sea. Just as you call on angels above, we are the angels below just below the surface. Call on us we will also help you are brothers and sisters.

Everything is an illusion in this world . . . Do you want to know what became of the Atlanteans? Well they became us the mer people. They are showing me this amazing underwater city; although it is anchored in the third dimension, is it not of the third dimension.

The mer people say that as humans we have forgotten how to live in the moment. Although they say we are getting somewhat better at it, there is still a ways to go. Enjoy everything that happens in the moment, then the next moment, and then the next moment. It is stringing the moments together, that creates your life and your story. This is how things connect not controlling, not planning, not plotting. It is about learning to flow, just like being in the water. As humans, you are too busy thinking and trying to figure everything out. There needs to be more play and more creativity.

They are showing me and teaching me how they travel in the streams or ley lines of the water. It is instantaneous. An example is when you go to a drive through bank and put your money in the tube. This is how they travel. They say there is a pressure in transportation and that soon we will be able to master under sea travel.

We as humans, with our deep-sea submarines and sonar, are threatening their way of life. As humans you thought you would be studying the ocean floor. However, you discovered whole universes that you cannot explain.

I am being shown the frequencies and way in which they use the water and light to communicate to other beings, planets and galaxies. Humans would describe it as rays of light.

The mer people are talking about the earth, they have a different perspective about land then we humans do. However, we are neglecting the water, which we are mostly made of. Because we breathe air for now and can't live under the water anymore, we do not see it as important as saving the land, however it is Justas important if not more so. We as humans are still made up of mostly water it is time we started to remember this.

I am being told the mer people our glad some of us our remembering and coming home. They have missed us and want to connect with their brothers and sisters.

The Elohim

From my perspective, The Elohim vibrate at a higher frequency then the Arch Angels and Ascended Masters. The Elohim hold and work with all the knowledge in the material universe. When I connect with The Elohim, I am brought up into a different dimension; a different frequency and a different vibration than what exists here on the 3rd dimensional earth plane. I am always left with a sense of awe and connection to everything that is.

The message and experience that came through: I am being shown and taken to a white and blue room. The Elohim I will always be safe here. They want us to know that when we see pictures from above whether it is from satellites, the space shuttle, or space station, it is one world, one planet, and one consciousness. Thinking humanity is separate because of countries and borders is how humanity stays stuck in fear. You are all human beings, living on planet earth together. Maybe this perspective needs to be the new focus and goal for humanity. From a global perspective, one planet, one group of beings. This concept of one humanity is going to become increasingly important in the next several years.

Plato

Plato was a philosopher and mathematician in Classical Greece. Tuning into this message, my brain actually hurt. It felt like it was above my level of cognition and yet somehow, I understood it at the same time.

This is the message that came through:

We may understand the mathematics that Plato left for us, however, we do not understand the spiritual human connection as of yet. That part got left out of the books and wisdom he left for us. Humanity needs to realize how powerful they are and develop a sense belonging to a bigger paradigm then just earth.

Our Sun

Have you ever looked up at the sun and feel like your eyes were burning? When the sun came through, that is how I felt. It felt like my whole body was burning up from the intensity. It was an amazing experience in retrospect; however it was difficult going through it.

This is the short message that came through:
This is a short message as it was a hard energy to hold for a prolonged period of time. Our sun aligns with the galactic sun, the power coming from what we think of as the sun. As our sun becomes more powerful and aligned, we become more aware and awake.

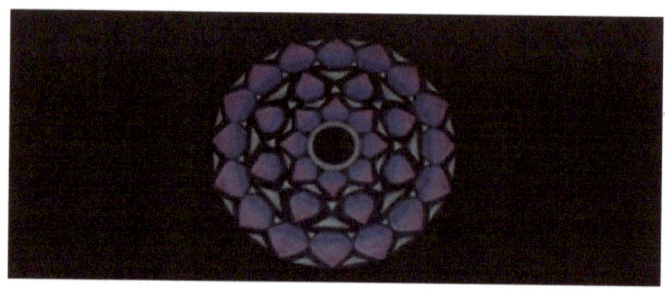

Ascended Master Kuan Yin

Ascended Master Kuan Yin is often thought of as the goddess of compassion and mercy. Ascended Master Kaun Yin is often depicted as having many arms. I have had the great honor to connect with all the ascended masters at different times. Kuan Yin's energy to me feels very gentle and compassionate. I feel like I am being held in a loving embrace that I never want to end.

This is the message that came through:
I am Kuan Yin. It is time for humans to remember love not fear. You need to come from a place in your heart, and be able to be transparent in the world. These were the messages many, many, many years ago. This is the energy seeded in the earth. This is what humanity needs to remember. It is about peace, community, love and joy. It is about creating the Garden of Eden on earth, not in some alternate reality. This can be a reality here now. Humanity needs to see that everything is connected. We are all one. What you do to yourself affects others and what you do to others affects yourself. This is the lesson humanity has forgotten, "compassion". This is why there are still so many wars, destruction. Humans have forgotten that what you put out comes back and hate will destroy all.

Indigenous People of the Earth Aborigines

When I connected with this energy, it felt very sacred. I felt like I was in an ancient ceremony with drums and didgeridoos, flutes and lots of dancing. It was an incredible event to witness and experience.

This is the message that came through:
We are the indigenous people of the earth. Ceremony and ritual are very important to us. Cycles and tides are very important. Humans need to become reacquainted with these. The fast paced world you live in now there is no time for this. It is really important to reconnect to nature, to tune and plug into the messages of the wind, the sun, the trees, and the rain forests. The rain forests need to stay intact or the earth will not be able to breathe, and then humans will not be able to breathe. If the rain forests that are left due not stay intact there will be major cataclysms on and in earth. It is imperative that you as human beings remember that you are connected to every living thing and every living thing is connected to you.

Mary Magdalene

When I connected with Mary Madeline I felt a soft, powerful force that was undeniable. There was this quiet power and strength that came through. The best way to describe it was motherly and maternal.

This is the message that came through:
I am Mary Magdalene; there is so much about me that has been untrue that I wanted to set the record straight. I as Jesus we are all about love, about being connected, about being one. We didn't need anyone else to believe what we believed. We just wanted people to feel better and be alive. We wanted to open people up. We were amongst human beings but not of the earth. We walked among human beings and also carried a lot of knowledge of where we come from and why we were here and what we were meant to do. The star was always looking out for us. Tit was our communication hub. We got help from above. As many on the planet now work with guides and multi dimensional beings, so did we.

In our times, the thing we did that you are learning to do as human beings now is living from your heart center. It is something that humans have forgotten for centuries, not living from the brain, not from the solar plexus, but from the heart. This is where miracles happen. Having heart connections with people is what allows one to have faith.

Every human being has a different frequency and vibration. Therefore, every human being has different guides and beings working with them. Often times, these guides and beings form electro magnetic force fields around you to help you to help you stay grounded, centered and focused.

So allow yourselves to feel it and take it in and realize that, you are always safe, and you are always loved. There are always guides looking out for you, guiding you and walking with you.

Ashtar of the Galactic Federation of the Light

Who is Ashtar? That is an awesome question. Whenever Ashtar comes through, I am always laughing. Ashtar always introduces himself saying this is "I am Ashtar of the Galactic Federation of the light". I think of Ashtar as a multi dimensional being that helps us on a planetary level with keeping humanity moving forward. I have had many experiences with Ashtar over the years. Before I get into the message I want to share one of the experiences.

When I was taking the Angelic Healing Fire class I had a private session. The instructor was doing some healing work with me. All of a sudden I heard this: " I am Ashtar of the Galactic Federation of the Light". Next thing I know Ashtar came in through my crown chakra and was in my body with me. This was a very strange experience to say the least. I was a little freaked out as this was the first time anything like this had ever happened. The instructor saw it as well. After awhile I told Ashtar he could not stay in my body with me. I told Ashtar, he could always be close by and he has been ever since.

This is the message that came through:

We are working with the grids of the earth right now. The energy is wonky right now. Everything feels out of sorts. Lessons are coming to the surface and people will chose to learn them and move forward or they will not and they will leave.

This is a point of no return. But we do it with love. We do it with kindness, and most importantly we do it with humor as this one resonates with humor and likes to laugh.

This is how she reaches people with her sense of humor. This is why all the clients have always felt comfortable with her.

Dolphins

When I experience dolphin energy, it feels similar to unicorn energy. I feel lighter and happier. I always look forward to when they come through. The dolphins are fifth dimensional beings left here to help humanity. Some say they are from Siria, I feel like they are more from the Pleiades. The truth is they can be from both.

This is the message and experience that came through:
You are moving into a new awareness of dimensions. You, as humans, are starting to see and believe how much we dolphins can help you.

The dolphins are taking me on a journey and showing me crystals and water made of crystals. It is nothing I have ever seen before. I am being taken into a pyramid structure, it feels amazing. I like it here. It is really cool. I just want to play with the dolphins going in and out of the pyramids.

The dolphins are now taking me to meet a being who keeps the pyramids. This being is full of magic like me the dolphins say. I am telepathically communicating with them. The dolphins say I am in the fifth dimension and I am seeing the pink and gold dolphins that have come to play with me. Their frequency is amazing and so pure.

The dolphins are communicating to me that I do not understand the scope of all my gifts yet and how magical I can really be. The dolphins are communicating that I really need to get back in touch with joy and play. When I am joyful and playful is when the magic will happen. Easily and effortlessly like spreading glitter . . .

There was another time in the beginning of my journey when my room filled with water and three dolphins came to play. They were pinging me with their sonar and we were having a whole telepathic conversation and I just felt so at home I did not want it to end.

Arch Angel Michael

Arch Angel Michael is the Arch Angel of Protection. I always feel safe and protected when I call on and/or work with Arch Angel Michael. Sometimes I see him all around me with his sword protecting me. Sometimes I call on his blue light to protect me.

The Message and Experiences with Arch Angel Michael:

Arch Angel Michael gave me a blue flame of truth. It runs through my whole body with an energetic sword. The sword of truth is an energetic gift to help me with others I come into contact with as a barometer; to what is ego and what is truth. When you tune into yourself, you will always know what is truth and what is ego. Unfortunately this has been really accurate and posed some interesting dilemmas for me when interacting with other human beings.

The sword of truth was given to me to help me discern what I should be putting my time and energy into and requests made of me. I Arch Angel Michael am here to help and learn how to use this flame of truth.

We have been with you before as well. They are showing me King Arthur and Knights of the Round Table and free masons. Some of what was given to King Arthur was lost in translation and some of it is still very accurate today.

There are times where you literally glow blue. I remember one time when the power went out for 26 hours I woke up in the middle of the night because there was this bright blue light, and it turned out it was me. That was even a little strange for me.

Ascended Master St Germain

Ascended Master St Germain gave us the violet flame. The flame can be used to transmute and purify energy. Ascended Master St Germain has a strong presence and leads me gently to where I need to go and what I need to figure out and sometimes what I need to let go of.

My experiences and messages from Ascended Master St Germain:

I was in a healing class with angels and we did a great deal of work with the violet flame. I found it to be very powerful and soothing at the same time. I have had a strong connection with the violet flame ever since and use it often. I am reminded that it is all around often as the violet flame or light shows up in many of my photographs.

Remember to call on me when you need help transmuting and letting go of things that no longer serve you.

Ascended Master Jesus:

Remember back to chapter one when I talked about the strength of my connection with Jesus? Some of you are going to consider this blasphemy, but sometimes I refer to him as the Buddy Christ, like in the movie Dogma. In my belief, Jesus actually has a sense of humor. Any way, I digressed there for a moment. In the beginning, I used to have all the stigmata pain, my hands/wrists, ankles, my right side and the crown of thorns digging into my head. My greatest fear would be that I would start bleeding from my wrists. Again I was working in a behavioral health (psychiatric) hospital at the time, and did I mention it was a Catholic facility? All I needed was to go into work with bandages around my wrists due to the bleeding that can occur with stigmata pain. I was so fearful about this. Although I continued to have the pain, I never did start bleeding and I was eternally grateful to my spirit team for not having to experience and/or explain that one to people.

I am going to wrap this chapter up with a list of blessings that were channeled from Jesus.
- May you always keep dreaming and reaching for the stars.

- May you always have faith in yourself and your gifts.
- May you always find peace, acceptance and clarity in yourself and your life.
- May you always use your voice and stand up for what you believe in.
- May you always believe you can make a difference - because you can.
- May you always have the strength and courage to be who you are meant to be regardless of what others think, do or say.
- May you always connect and live through your heart.
- May you always follow your bliss.
- May you always learn to bend, flex and live in the flow.
- May you always fully accept and love yourself, as you are – a divine spark.
- May you always be true to yourself.
- May you always be full of joy, laughter, spontaneity and awe.
- May you always be in peace and grace.
- May you always be able to receive that which is present for you.
- May you always be awake and make conscious choices.
- May you always have the power to live fully in the moment.
- May you always be who you are with confidence.
- May you always have something to cherish and be grateful for every day.
- May you always be able to count your blessings.

- May you always let go of regret, guilt and shame and be in the present moment.
- May you always be blessed with friends who love you for you.
- May you always know how loved and cared for you truly are every minute of every day, because you are.
- May you always have inner peace and contentment.
- May you always be true to yourself and dance to the beat of your soul.

Section Four:
Meditations and Prayer

Chakra Wash

First imagine yourself lying down on a massage table. Now like a car wash, the table you are on slowly moves forward and a series of three Red Lights first go vertically over your body starting at the top of your head over the front of you all the way down your toes then the lights go under the table and go from your feet to the top of your head.

This process happens 3 times.

Then the are seven red lights and they align with each chakra (energy Center) and they go around your body three times and you feel completely saturated with red light. Lie here for a while and let the beautiful red light just course through your body.

Now you feel the massage table being moved and there are three orange lights that start at the top of your head and go down to your toes and under the table and from your toes to the top of your head.

Now, seven orange lights come on and align with each charka and go around your body three times. You lay here and feel the amazing glow of the orange and feel totally at peace with yourself and who you are.

Now the massage table moves again and a series of three yellow lights that start at the top of your head and go down to your toes and under the table and from your toes to the top of your head.

Now, the seven yellow lights come on and align with each charka and go around your body three times. You lay here and feel the amazing glow of the yellow light and feel at peace with your own power and realize that you will use your power for the highest good.

Again the massage table moves and now there is a series of three green and pink lights that start at the top of your head and go down to your toes and under the table and from your toes to the top of your head.

Now, the seven green lights come on and align with each charka and go around your body three times. You lay here and feel the amazing strength of living in your heart and feeling connected to all that is.

Again the massage table moves and you feel the glow of three light blue lights that start at the top of your head and go down to your toes and under the table and from your toes to the top of your head.

Now, the seven light blue lights come on and align with each charka and go around your body three times. You lay here and feel that you will be able to go out in the world and speak your truth with conviction and love.

The massage table moves again and you see three indigo lights that start at the top of your head and go down to your toes and under the table and from your toes to the top of your head.

Now, the seven indigo lights come on and align with each charka and go around your body three times. You lay here and realize you are open to your intuition and any messages that may come through, whether you see, hear, feel or just know.

You know that these messages are truth and you no longer fight them but allow them to flow with ease.

The massage table moves again and you see three violet lights that start at the top of your head and go down to your toes and under the table and from your toes to the top of your head.

Now, the seven violet lights come on and align with each charka and go around your body three times. You lay here and feel the connection with the divine and realize (real – eyes) that we are all one and are all part of the whole. You feel completely enveloped in love, peace, joy, harmony and bliss.

The massage table moves one last time and you are now surround in a rainbow light bath and just soak up any last minute rays that you need to take with you. You are welcome to come back to your chakra wash any time that you need to be refreshed or nourished.

Take a couple of minutes and write down any feelings, sensations, insights that you may have felt while doing this activity.

Meditation for Balance and Alignment

Close your eyes and take a couple of deep breaths. Breathe in through your nose and out through your mouth. Once you have slowed down and are feeling in a more peaceful place. You are ready to begin.

There is a red triangle that is spinning over your head about two feet bigger than your physical body is. This red triangle moves down over your crown chakra, over your third eye chakra, your throat chakra, your heart chakra, your solar plexus chakra, your sacral chakra and lands and locks in at your root chakra. Once the red triangle hits your root chakra it starts to spin at the rate, vibration and speed you need to balance, align, clear, cleanse, heal, and harmonize your root chakra.

There is now an orange triangle spinning over your head and again is two feet bigger than your physical body. The orange triangle moves down over your crown chakra, over your third eye chakra, your throat chakra, your heart chakra, your solar plexus chakra, and lands at your sacral chakra and locks in. Once the orange triangle hits your sacral chakra it starts to spin at the rate, vibration and speed you need it to balance, align, clear, cleanse, heal and harmonize your sacral chakra.

There is now a yellow triangle spinning over your head and again it is two feet bigger than your physical body. The yellow triangle moves down over your crown chakra, over your third eye chakra, your throat chakra, your heart chakra, and lands at your solar plexus chakra and locks in. One the yellow triangle hits your solar plexus chakra it starts to spin at the rate, vibration and speed you need to balance align, clear, cleanse, heal and harmonize your solar plexus chakra.

There is now a green triangle spinning over your ahead. Again it is two feel bigger than your physical body. The green triangle moves down over your crown chakra, over your third eye chakra, your throat chakra lands and locks in to your heart chakra. One the green triangle locks in, it starts to spin at the rate, vibration and speed you need to balance, align, clear, cleanse heal and harmonize your heart chakra.

There is now a light blue triangle spinning over your head. Again it is two feet bigger than your physical body. The light blue triangle moves down over your crown chakra, over your third eye chakra and lands and locks in at your throat chakra. Once the light blue triangle locks in it starts to spin at the rate, vibration and speed you need to balance, align, clear, cleanse heal, and harmonize your throat chakra.

There is now an indigo blue triangle spinning over your head. Again it is two feet bigger than your physical body. The indigo blue triangle moves over crown chakra, lands and locks in on your third eye chakra. One the indigo blue triangle is locked in it starts to spin at the rate, vibration and speed you need to balance, align, clear, cleanse, heal and harmonize your third eye chakra.

There is now a white and purple triangle spinning over your head. Again it is two feet bigger than your physical body. The white and purple triangle moves over crown chakra, lands and locks in on your crown chakra. Once the white and purple triangle is locked in it starts to spin at the rate, vibration and speed you need to balance, align, clear, cleanse, heal and harmonize your crown chakra.

Now take a minute and feel all the triangles spinning at your chakras . . . Let it all sink in. They are all spinning at a different, rate, vibration and frequency.

When you are ready take a couple of deep breaths and come back, ground and reorient yourself to your surroundings.

Take a few minutes to journal about the experience. What did it bring up for you? What did it feel like? Was there a triangle and color that was more difficult to work with? Was there a triangle and color that was especially easy for you to work with? Did you get any messages about what is going on in your body?

Chakra Meditation with Mandalas

Sit comfortably. Take some deep breaths. Breathe in through your nose out through your mouth.

Gaze at the root chakra image.

Imagine that this root chakra image is transposed onto your root chakra at the base of your spine. Allow your root chakra to fill with beautiful red light and divine red energy. Feel your root chakra clear, cleanse heal, harmonize, balance and align.

Take some deep breaths and all the energy to swirl. . .

Gaze at the sacral chakra image.

Imagine that that the sacral chakra image is transposed onto your sacral chakra, which is half way between the base of your spine and your belly button. Allow your sacral chakra to fill with beautiful orange light and divine orange energy. Feel your sacral chakra clear, cleanse heal, harmonize, balance and align.

Take some deep breaths and allow the energy to swirl...

Gaze at the solar plexus chakra image.

Imagine that this solar plexus chakra image is transposed onto your solar plexus chakra in your stomach area. Allow your solar plexus chakra to fill with beautiful yellow light and divine yellow energy. Feel your solar plexus chakra clear, cleanse heal, harmonize, balance and align.

Take some deep breaths and allow the energy to swirl. . .

Gaze at the heart chakra image.

Imagine that this heart chakra image is transposed onto your heart chakra. Allow your heart chakra to fill with beautiful green and pink light and divine green and pink energy. Feel your heart chakra clear, cleanse heal, harmonize, balance and align.

Take some deep breaths and allow the energy to swirl. . .

Gaze at the throat chakra image.

Imagine that this throat chakra image is transposed onto your throat chakra. Allow your throat chakra to fill with beautiful light blue light and divine light blue energy. Feel your throat chakra clear, cleanse heal, harmonize, balance and align.

Take some deep breaths and allow the energy to swirl. . .

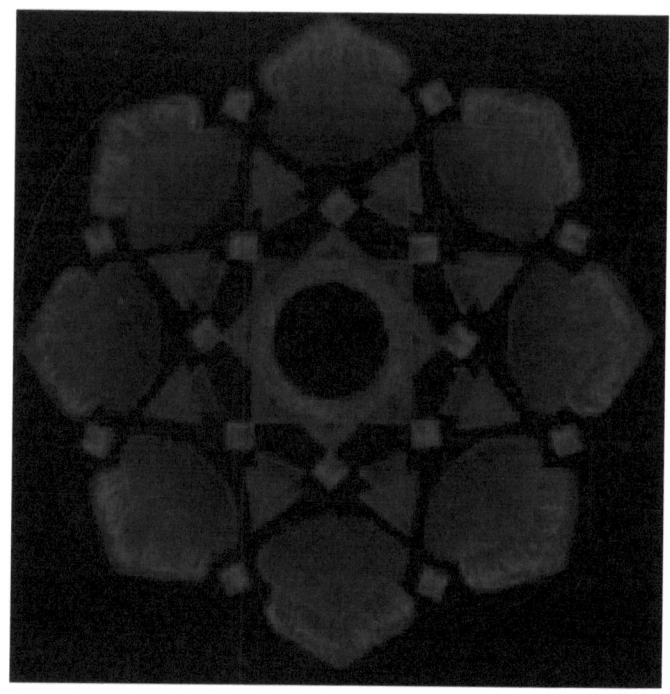

Gaze at the third eye chakra image.

Imagine that the third eye chakra image is transposed onto your third eye chakra, which is in the middle of your forehead. Allow your third eye chakra to fill with beautiful indigo blue light and divine indigo blue energy. Feel your third eye chakra clear, cleanse heal, harmonize, balance and align.

Take some deep breaths and allow the energy to swirl. . .

Gaze at the crown chakra image.

Imagine that this crown chakra image is transposed onto your crown chakra at the top of your head. Allow your crown chakra to fill with beautiful white, silver and violet light and divine white, silver and violet energy. Feel your crown chakra clear, cleanse heal, harmonize, balance and align.

Take some deep breaths and allow the energy to swirl. . . .

Gaze at the synergy image.

This image is filled with the energy of all the chakras.

Imagine that the synergy image starts at your crown chakra at the top of your head, and fills your crown chakra with rainbow light and divine rainbow energy.

The synergy image moves down to your third eye chakra in the middle of your forehead filling your third eye with rainbow light and divine rainbow energy.

The synergy image continues to move down to your throat chakra filling your throat chakra with rainbow light and divine rainbow energy, and now moves down to your heart chakra filling your heart chakra with rainbow light and divine rainbow energy moving down to your solar plexus, filling your solar plexus with rainbow light and divine rainbow energy the synergy image continues down to your sacral chakra filling it with rainbow light and divine rainbow energy and moving down to your root chakra filling your root chakra with rainbow light and divine rainbow energy.

Now send the synergy image, rainbow light and divine rainbow energy all the way down to mother earth. Allow mother earth to send up grounding energy to help you stabilize, balance, clear, cleanse, and stay healed and aligned.

Meditation to get your own symbol

Close your eyes and take a couple deep breaths. Breathe deeply in through your nose, out through your mouth. Let everything else fall away as you focus on breathing.

Imagine yourself in a beautiful garden, can be a meadow, the beach, a waterfall garden, rock garden, and English meadow… It can be an actual place. Allow whatever image pops up to continue. Take in the sights and sounds of your landscape.

See if there are other people, animals, flowers, colors, and smells…Let it all permeate your senses. As you continue to walk through the landscape you have created you start to see a house, it has seven steps and a pink door.

You start to walk toward the house. As you approach the house you step on the first step and it lights up red. You step up on the second step and it lights up orange. You step up to the third step and it lights up yellow. You step up onto the fourth step and it lights up green. You step up onto the fifth step and it lights up light blue. You step up on the sixth step and it lights up indigo blue. You step up onto the seventh step it lights up white.
You have now reached the pink door.

You enter the pink door and are in a room flooded with violet and gold light and see that there are two chairs sitting there. You make your way towards the chairs and sit down. Now sitting across from you is a guide, loved one, angel ascended master or light being who is going to assist you and give you your symbol which you will be able to remember and recreate when you return. You may ask the being sitting across from you any questions you would like and greet them in way that you like. Once they are sitting across from you they will give you the symbol to create. When you are ready you will thank the being for coming and embrace them in any way you would like.

You now get up and go through the pink door. You are standing on the white seventh step, which unlights. You step down to the sixth step the indigo step and it unlights. You step down to the fifth step the light blue step and it unlights. You step down to the fourth step the green step and it unlights. You step down to the third step the yellow step and it unlights. You step down to the second step the orange step and it unlights. You step down to the first step the red step and it unlights. Now you are back in your landscape you take a few minutes looking around reorienting your self.

When you are ready you can open your eyes and sketch or just start drawing your symbol.

Perhaps you would like to take a few minutes to journal about the experience, such as who came to see you? What your landscape was like? Or about how you felt during the experience.

Prayer before creating images

Prayer I say before creating any image:

I am opening to receiving with love.
Thank you for Blessing me with your presence and grace.
I allow you to flow through me to create for the highest good of _____.
May our hearts be one for now and always.
Namaste!

Epilogue

Putting this book together caused me to have to work through a great deal of personal fear and judgment. Throughout the whole process the thoughts that kept going through my head were could I really put this out there? What are other people going to think? Will I ever be able to get another job as a therapist based on some of the things I have disclosed in this book? Lastly, can and should I publish using my real name?

Then I reread the channeling section of the book. It is funny how things come together. When I was transcribing the hours of messages, many of which were for me personally as well as for humanity; I knew at this point that I had to put this information out there and I had to use my name. This is who I am after all, someone that stirs it up and follows my own intuition and guidance. I dance to the beat of my own drum, so to speak. The messages that I took away are we all need to be and live in flow, in the moment and from our own hearts. We are one race, the human race. We are all living together on one planet, Earth. Earth (the world) needs all of us to be who we are meant to be and fulfill our destiny and walk our path.

I am hoping now that you have read my experiences and messages we can start an honest conversations about experiences everyone is having. I am not the only one having these types of metaphysical experiences. It is time to break the taboo and stop thinking about what others are going to think of you and be the most authentic you, you can be. Life is short. We are not here for that long in the grand scheme of things. It is time to take your place in the global world. Step away from fear and move into love and living from your heart space. None of us are getting out alive. Just something you may want to remember.

Thank you for allowing me to share my journey with you. It has been a privilege and honor. Thank you also for keeping an open mind while reading this. I know some of it was extremely strange and weird. This is what happened to me. Now let's start the conversation about what is happening with you.

Namaste!

www.ingramcontent.com/pod-product-compliance
Lightning Source LLC
Chambersburg PA
CBHW042050290426
44110CB00001B/16